"MEAN"
JOE GREENE
BUILT BY FOOTBALL

JOE GREENE

WITH JON FINKEL

Front Cover designed by: Kinsey Stewart
Edited by: Scott Bedgood

ISBN: 978-0-9986273-0-4

A FOOTBALLMATTERS.ORG PUBLICATION

Presented by:

The National Football Foundation &

College Football Hall of Fame

"MEAN"
JOE GREENE
BUILT BY FOOTBALL

FOREWORD

By: Franco Harris

For nearly 40 years, the Pittsburgh Steelers were at the bottom of the professional football world. The one benefit of being at the bottom is that you get a high pick in the first round of the next year's NFL draft. As any football fan will tell you, draft picks are hit or miss...and the Steelers mostly missed. Then, in 1969, the Steelers selected a player out of North Texas that the reporters initially called "Joe Who?" Well, it didn't take long for those very same reporters to remember the name "Mean" Joe Greene.

On his first day of training camp, Joe started to

chart the course for the future. His first order of business was to bring a new outlook to the team and the city that can be summed up like this: losing was no longer acceptable. And just like that, the fate of the Steelers would lie in his big hands.

Joe quickly pushed the Steelers in a new direction with a new mindset. He demanded a lot of himself and of his teammates. By the time I was drafted a few years later, it was clear that Joe was the cornerstone of our team. With him in place, the Steelers drafted players to fit this new system and mentality. The results are now legendary, as we won four Super Bowls and the Steelers became the new standard of professional football.

Yes, Joe was the spark that ignited it all, and as time passes, his role continues to shine brighter and brighter. There is no question in my mind that "Mean" Joe Greene is the greatest Steeler of all time!

FOREWORD
By: Dan Rooney

Joe Greene is a special person. From the day he arrived at St. Vincent College, his impact was noticed by everyone. Joe took on the entire offensive line. Chuck Noll noticed Joe's ability and leadership skills. Joe went on to be a true standout person.

One season we were in Philadelphia playing the Eagles. We were losing by a short margin, and trying hard to maintain control of the ball. At one point, Joe showed his frustration by throwing the ball into the stands. Many complained that he was being unsportsmanlike. I said, "No, Joe will do whatever it takes to win."

Joe was always involved. One time, when we played the Oilers, our defense was really hurt. In the beginning of the game, Joe immediately made five tackles. He brought the other players to a higher level.

I remember Joe as being unique, as did my father. Joe and Terry Bradshaw often enjoyed smoking cigars in my father's office. These were great times – a great team.

Joe always did what he thought was necessary. He was still a young man when we became the team of the decade in the 70s. He had many achievements, playing in Super Bowls, Pro Bowls, and all the best recognitions. He was enshrined in the Pro Football Hall of Fame in 1987. However, he was not interested in the accolades. He was focused on being the best.

You might remember him being in the great Coca-Cola commercial. It was voted the best commercial of the year. It is a true classic.

Joe continued his great career with the NFL after his time as a player. He was an assistant coach with the Steelers for four years, then with Miami and Arizona. Later he joined the Steelers Scouting department, and continued to make important contributions to the team. He always motivated the players to do their best.

Joe has been a good father to his three children, a good husband, and it has been wonderful to have Joe as a representative of the Steelers in all the ways he was involved with the team.

Joe will always be known as an outstanding member of the NFL.

INTRODUCTION

I've done countless interviews about the Steel Curtain defense and our Super Bowl wins in Pittsburgh
and the famous Coca-Cola commercial and I've been
forthcoming about my feelings in regards to all of
them.

There have been so many documentaries and stories
written on those subjects that plenty of information
is out there online and in print for those who want to
study up on those topics. I don't want to be redun-
dant here.

What excites me about publishing a book like this, in
a format where I can talk about what football has
meant to me, is that I can cover many of the topics

that I haven't had the opportunity to discuss, because the truth is, I didn't play football so I could make commercials.

I didn't play football so people could see me and know me.

I played for the joy of being out there on the field.

When I was nine or ten years old we didn't even keep score. We played pick-up games in the street with no coaches and no scoreboard and nobody telling us what to do or not do. The games ended when it got too dark to play.

Many times during my peak years in Pittsburgh I thought about how great it would be if I could play the games on Sunday and fight my battles on the field with my teammates and then, after soaking in a hard-fought win, I could somehow walk off the field and become a small one-hundred-and-fifty pound guy and blend into the crowd.

That's my real personality. I'm a naturally shy guy.

Football forced me to overcome that and prevented me from withdrawing into myself. It made me want to be a part of a team. It helped me understand the concepts of teamwork and respect. It also taught me that treating others with respect required the right mindset.

You have to respect yourself, your teammates, your coaches, your family, your high school, your college, your organization and on up the chain. It's an ongoing process and I was lucky enough to learn from some great men during my playing days.

This was especially important to me because I was raised by a single mother and the male influences in my life as a young man were all coaches. There are aspects about life and life lessons that can only be learned when a young man spends his time day-in and day-out with a strong role model. I had that with Coach Rod Rust at North Texas and Coach Chuck Noll in Pittsburgh.

Later on in my career, as a scout for the Steelers, I came across so many kids that were in the same shoes I had been in. Kids with just a mother or grandmother involved in their life. Kids with just an auntie. Kids living with their coaches.

The only strong male influences in these boys' lives were the men they encountered through football. And one of the reasons the game is so important to me is because of what it did for me and what it can do for young men who find themselves in the situation I was in. Not only do you learn how to become a man, how to behave and how to be responsible for yourself and for others, but you get, in my view, an instant response to your efforts, or your lack of effort. You get instant nullification or gratification in what you do.

What does that mean?

It means that if you don't put in the time and you don't put in the effort necessary to achieve something, then the end result is not going to be something that you like. It means that if you take a play off you end up on your back. It's instant feedback on whether you put in enough work and energy to succeed. Real life is like that, too.

In some ways, the adversity you experience on a football field, physically and mentally, gives you a sense of how deep you can dig to battle back. How badly do you want to win? What are you willing to endure?

In that regard, football helped show me what I was made of.

When I got to North Texas I was rough around the edges as a man and as a player. College helped polish me up a bit and then when I got to Pittsburgh my teammates helped me to continue to smooth things out. I'm a better person because of the men who coached me and the men I played with. I learned from all of them. I'd like to take this opportunity to pass along that knowledge.

CONTENTS

BUILT BY FOOTBALL

CHAPTER 1
ALWAYS PICKED LAST

Depending on which one of my buddies was captain of our pick-up games, I was either chosen last or dead last. There was another kid that was built like me and looked like me and we basically rotated who was the last boy taken.

This scene played itself out over and over again throughout my football-playing childhood. I can still picture it. We'd be on the schoolyard or at a park or in the streets of Temple, Texas, where I grew up, and all of the kids would gather in a group and we'd choose two captains and then they'd start taking kids one by one. It was a sort of natural selection that followed the same pattern every game, where the fastest guys would be taken first, and then the middle kids who were a little fast, and then the slow kids...and then me and this other guy would wait to see who would be taken last.

I was slow and maybe a little chunky and I'd say more often than not the honor of being picked last fell to me. I don't remember being mad about it in any way because that's just how it was. I would have taken the fast kids too, especially the kid who was always taken first. He was younger than me but he was exceptionally quick. Watching him play made me understand that some people are just born fast and I wasn't one of them.

I was a big kid, though. By seventh grade I was tall and well over 150 pounds. On a scale of one-to-ten of being a good athlete, I'd have to say I was a zero. I was terrible at every sport.

I was so bad at basketball it's barely even worth talking about because I refused to play once I saw how awful I was. Also, back then basketball players wore those short shorts, and I know it's a funny thing to talk about now, but I was a self-conscious kid and I was very uncomfortable wearing the shorts.

They were tight and it felt like my thighs were going to explode in them and that my butt was coming out of them and I remember thinking, "I can't go out in front of the other students like this."

So you combine that with the fact that I stunk and it discouraged me from playing.

When it came to baseball I was scared of the ball. It's the truth. As soon as the pitcher would release the pitch I'd be halfway to the dugout to get out of the way. I played little league but I could never get used to it. Then when I was a freshman in high school the coach wanted to make me a pitcher and I walked every single batter I faced. That didn't last long. I was embarrassed. I ended up finishing out the season as the batboy for the varsity team.

And that left football. I may have been slow, but I loved to play and I went out for the freshman team as soon as I got to high school.

The coach was an old school guy and in his mind if you were big you played fullback, so that's what I started out as.

My career as a running back lasted about one game. In fact, I remember my last play as a back, 26 Spinner.

Ohhhh, I'll never forget 26 Spinner!

The play was kind of like a counter, where as the running back, I'd start out one way while the quarterback started out another after the snap. Then he'd spin back and I'd reverse direction and he'd hand me the ball. I remember the play working out fine in practice, but our first game was against a powerhouse team from Austin, Texas called Austin Anderson. They were a Class AAA all-black school, and to say they took us behind the woodshed and whipped our butts would be an understatement.

Our coach called 26 Spinner a bunch of times that game and I never made it out of the backfield. Not once.

Needless to say, after that performance I was moved to guard and then also defensive tackle.

Once again, I wasn't very good.

One of my best friends was our middle linebacker. We were the same age and had been playing together for a long time. In my first game as a tackle I got knocked off the ball nearly every play and he would get his clock cleaned because the other team's lead blocker would get a clear shot at him. He was fussing at me the whole game and I couldn't blame him. I was missing tackles and he was getting creamed. I'd have been upset too!

I suffered from a complete and total lack of confidence both on the field and in my personal life. In fact, it was during this time, say from 6th grade to my sophomore year in high school that I was bullied nonstop.

***

When I was in middle school and it was time to go home, I'd have to take little peaks out the front door of the school to see if anyone was waiting out there to beat me up. If someone was waiting for me I'd do the same thing to the side door of the school.

I'd crack it open a sliver and peer out or I'd lean back behind one of the windows to see if I could spot anyone. If the coast was clear, I'd leave. If not, I'd try the back door.

If people were waiting for me I'd hang around school a bit until I saw an opening to leave, and the second I did, I was running the moment I hit the pavement to get home as fast as I could so the bullies wouldn't see me.

Remember, I wasn't very fast at the time. If they saw me they'd surely catch me. I can still recall that feeling I'd have in the pit of my stomach when school would end and I'd begin scouting out the best way to leave. It was an awful, helpless sensation. And it wasn't like the kids bullying me wanted to seriously hurt me. It was just fighting. They never broke any bones or anything, but I was a big guy and they just wanted to brag that they took me down. Basically, they wanted to humiliate me and it didn't feel good at all.

The ringleader of the bullying was a guy who was actually my friend some of the time. His name was Speedy. He was a few years older than me and we were about the same size, but he would mercilessly tease me and beat me up. It happened no matter what we did.

If we played pick-up basketball or football or baseball or whatever it was he'd always want to play against me and he'd whoop me. I was ashamed that I couldn't stop him.

To this day I remember one of the most embarrassing moments of my life, courtesy of Speedy.

It happened when I was in 8th grade and we were at the high school basketball game. I was sitting down in one of the front rows with a few cute girls and I was flirting with them, having a good time. Well, of course Speedy is sitting in the back, taunting me and then, as I'm talking to the girls, he uses a rubber band and flings a wet wad of paper at me and it pops me on the side of the head.

The entire gym started laughing at me, including the girls I was flirting with. In eighth grade getting embarrassed like that in front of a girl you like is just about one of the worst things that can happen to you.

But you know what's even worse? Not only did I not stand up for myself... I didn't even turn around because I knew it was Speedy who threw the paper and I didn't want to get in a fight with him in front of everyone because he'd beat me up. It was a gut-wrenching moment. I had to just walk out, ashamed.

This bullying lasted a few years and finally came to a head when I was a sophomore. One of the final incidents I had with Speedy involved football.

Like I said earlier, the worst part about the bullying from Speedy was that half of the time he acted like my friend, so I never knew where he was coming from if he came around and I was always on edge.

One day right before our sophomore football season, a few friends came by my house to pick me up to go shoot some pool. Speedy was with them and he actually came into my house. Now at the time, parents had to pay insurance for their kids to play football, so my mom had left five dollars on top of the TV set for me to bring into school the next day.

Well we all go play pool for a while and everything is fine. I get home, go to bed, and then the next morning when I went to grab the money before practice it was gone.

I had one thought in my head.

Speedy took it.

I was furious. My mom worked all the time to pay for things like that for me and this guy comes in my house and just steals her hard-earned money?

I was so mad I walked over to Speedy's house after school and pounded on his door until he answered.

"What do you want?" he said.

"Speedy, the five dollars that my mom left on top of the television for my football insurance... Did you take it?" I asked.

"Yeah, I took it," he said. "What are you going to do about it?"

Bam!

I hit him. Right there in his house. I didn't even think about it.

I hit him and hit him and knocked him to the ground and kept on hitting him until he was on the ground covering himself up and I decided to stop.

When I left he was still on the ground. He wasn't hurt badly or anything but he was down. I had finally snapped and fought back.

And what happened next is what you always hear about in those situations, which is that the next time I saw him he didn't mess with me at all. He acted like nothing happened.

Then, one by one, whenever the other guys who picked on me came around to mess with me I'd beat them up too.

I went from being the victim for many years, to not taking it anymore, to becoming the bully myself. I quit running and started fighting back and things changed fast. I just decided that I'd beat them to the punch in the literal sense. If you were walking up to me to mess with me you were gonna get hit. Guys stopped walking up to me. I never got beat up again.

***

Shortly after my confrontation with Speedy I started dating a girl who I really liked. When we started dating she hadn't been to any football games yet and up to that point, I was still getting my butt handed to me all over the field. I don't know if I gained confidence from confronting Speedy or I was just a guy who didn't want his girlfriend to see him get pushed around on the football field, but something clicked inside of me and I decided to be a more aggressive player.

Couple that with the fact that I was moved to middle linebacker, which felt freeing to me after being stuck on the line for so long, and it was like a new beginning. Suddenly, I worked harder on my running and I grew into my body a bit and I could run sideline to sideline with a little speed. Plus, I was still a big kid. I was about 6'1" and 230 pounds playing middle linebacker as a sophomore.

When you added up my motivation to play better with my new aggressive attitude and a new sense of my abilities, well, I finally started to have some success on the football field.

That success began to breed confidence and, pretty soon, I began to believe that whatever confrontation I got into on the football field I'd win. Now this isn't to say I was cocky at all. That's never been my personality. Even after my confrontation with Speedy I was quiet and withdrawn. I've never been the kind to pound my chest for being successful. In fact, I often downplayed my success because I was uncomfortable with the attention.

I was never comfortable having all eyes on me. I wasn't the life of the party or the guy who could tell a joke to make everyone laugh or the guy who would carry on a great conversation. I remember when I was a junior or senior I was terrified because the coaches made me a captain and that meant that I was going to have to speak in front of the team or in front of the school at homecoming and I didn't want any part of that.

Basically, I was becoming two different people: one on the football field and one off.

While I was an introvert off the field, once I put on my uniform I was going to play to win, and that meant playing as hard as I could on every down to get after the ball. I disregarded offensive lineman, blockers, anyone who got in my way. That was my mindset. I had a singular, focused intensity every single play.

The thing that I was learning simultaneously was that even though I had somewhat found myself as a football player, I was still only one man on a team of forty-plus guys and we were not a very good team.

I did what I could to win my individual battles, but I don't think we finished above .500 in any year of my high school career. But while I wasn't learning how to win, I was learning all kinds of other skills that I would take with me throughout my career.

One of the main things I began to understand as a player is that you have to decide what kind of fuel you are going to use when you play. This is also something that I talked about with my players when I was a coach.

Like I said, once I stepped foot on that field and understood that I was capable of beating whoever tried to block me, I had to manage my intensity.

The analogy I used with my players was that you could either have jet fuel or diesel fuel. Jet fuel burns faster and is explosive. Diesel is slow but it has power. Well, I'd rather play with jet fuel. That's mentally how I'd rather be and how I'd want my players to be.

You have to be fast and explosive. When you make contact you want to blow up the other person. You don't have time to be slow.

Another analogy I liked comes from the animal kingdom and it involves a lion and a gazelle. The lion wakes up every day and he's prowling around, looking for food like a gazelle to eat. The gazelle wakes up knowing the lion is out there trying to eat him, so he isn't prowling around, he's ready to haul ass whenever he needs to so he isn't eaten by the lion.

The football field is like that jungle. It's no place to be cool. You're hunting or being hunted. You're either the lion or the gazelle. You can survive as either one, but you need to know what fuel to use when. This is not something that young men learn easily, me included. It takes times and training and patience. It also helps to have coaches and teammates around you who will help you learn when to go all out and when to throttle back a bit.

As you'll see, it took me a while to get my fuel and my energy under wraps.

CHAPTER 2
OUT OF CONTROL

Desire, hustle and fight.

I had several coaches in high school but Coach Lester Moore stands out as the one who had the most influence on me. His number one goal was to put the fight in you and to teach you to outhustle the other guy. One of his gifts was that he motivated you in a way that made you want to succeed for him. He was constantly throwing fuel on your fire.

He had a few sayings that he repeated over and over again and one of them I can still hear him saying to this day. It's a pretty common phrase in football and life that I've heard many times since, but I heard it

31

first from him over 50 years ago, so it sticks in my head as coming from him. The saying is, "It ain't the size of the dog in the fight, but the size of the fight in the dog."

He used to say that to us every single day and it worked because we needed the motivation, especially in summer practices. I say this because while we all loved football, our facilities certainly weren't anything to brag about. We could have used some major upgrades.

For one, our field was nice and grassy for about three days and then it was nothing but dirt for the rest of the season. Our locker rooms were tight and musty. None of our pads or helmets were new. Our shoes might have been new for some guys, but pretty soon they were worn out or soaked through with dirt and mud and it was very common for us to have blisters from practicing twice a day in that hundred-degree heat in late August and early September.

Believe me, there were plenty of days that you wanted to quit, but you wouldn't.

Then we had all these other restrictions to teach us discipline and focus. The two big ones were no cigarettes and no beer. The other one was that you couldn't be seen with a girl the day before a game or on game day. The idea was that the game was too important to lose focus or get in trouble.

Of course, there was also a pretty rough punishment to go along with enforcing those rules.

If somebody saw you drinking a beer or taking a pull on a cigarette or with your girlfriend the morning of a game, you had to roll.

Man, I still wince thinking about it.

Rolling is when you start on the goal line, lying prone on the ground, with your hands behind your head. Then you roll over and over again as fast as you can until the coach says to stop. We'd need a spotter so that you didn't roll in a circle. By the time coach would tell you to stop, maybe 50 or 100 yards later, there was a 90% chance that you'd throw up when you stood up.

That was our punishment and it was too harsh for me, so I didn't mess around with those rules.

I did, however, have a problem with my temper back then and I got thrown out of almost every single high school game I played in my junior and senior year. It's not something I'm proud of in any way, but I struggled with it my entire career.

For some reason, it took me so long to understand that my behavior was hurting my team. It wasn't until I was with the Steelers when one day, Coach Noll pulled me aside after I unloaded on an official and he said to me very calmly, "You know, Joe, those officials are human beings too. They have families and they probably don't like being talked to like that."

I don't know why, but after years of acting out, what Coach Noll said really sunk in. For so long I had a real strong dislike for officials. I looked at them as people who didn't have anything invested in the game but who could determine its outcome. When they made mistakes, it costs us yards and sometimes those yards could cost us a win. I knew how hard we were working to get a win and I resented them for being in a position to determine the out-come of a ballgame.

In high school I was very immature. I constantly ar-gued with officials. Part of it was a total lack of personal control on my end and the other part was that we lost all the time. I hated losing and we lost almost all of our games, so after I'd hit someone on the other side of the ball and I had no one left to hit, I'd yell at the refs.

I know the coaches tried to talk to me in the begin-ning but I was so young I didn't listen. My attitude was, "get out of here with that". I didn't even give any thought to trying to control it. It was just part of me and I took that angry attitude into every game.

In fact, I began to develop a bad reputation around our league. People used to talk about how there was a good-sized kid from Temple, Texas who had an at-titude and wasn't afraid to take people out.

I remember one incident when we played Waco Carver where I really took someone down. They had an excellent wide receiver who was also a track star and they ran all kinds of plays for him. On this particular play, I could see a reverse developing so I sprinted to where I believed he was going to end up with the ball, near their sideline.

Well, I was right and just as he was coming around the outside corner, when he thought he was free and clear, I came around the edge and knocked him clear off the field into the tower that was holding up the lights on the sideline. Luckily he wasn't seriously hurt, but I caused two things with that play.

The first was that my team became very emotional and excited from the play.

The second was that I got booed loudly.

It was a clean hit, as I recall, but the ferocity of it and the visual of him bouncing off a light tower was enough to cement my reputation. Of course, we didn't win the game and my bad attitude continued.

The follow-up to that story comes a year later, when I maybe hit the low point of my behavior in high school.

Back then, when teams would travel, after the games they would eat at a local diner before they drove home. After our game my senior year, I happened to show up at the diner in Temple that the team we had just lost to was eating in.

I remember I was still burning from losing that game and through the window I could see these guys having a great time, eating burgers, eating fries, laughing at how bad they beat us.

I watched them all, fuming, until they left.

As they filed out, one of the kids who was gloating about winning walked by me eating an ice cream. Something possessed me at that moment and I took the cone from him and rubbed it all over his face. He was stunned and he ran across the street where his bus was and I chased him down. I got closer and closer until he squeezed on the bus and slammed the door right before I got there.

I wedged my fingers in the door and pulled it open to continue going after the kid. I had become possessed. I'll never forget that someone threw a soda bottle at me, but it missed and shattered the door as I was opening it. I wasn't even fazed. I was so out of control that I didn't even stop to think that I was forcing my way onto a bus with an entire team of football players who just whipped my school's butt.

What was even more incredible is that when I forced the door open the team streamed out the back of the bus. None of them wanted anything to do with me. I never chased the kids out back and pretty soon I was standing on the other team's bus by myself. It was an incredible incident.

When my coaches found out they were not happy. In the next game they told me that if I started that kind of crap on the field again they were going to let the other team beat me up if they came after me.

Sure enough, I started a bunch of crap and the other team piled on me. And true to their word, my coaches didn't step in.

I know it was hard on Coach Moore because I think deep down he loved my toughness and intensity and attitude on the field, but he didn't like me getting thrown out and starting fights and racking up penalties. The problem was that I was a good player, so me not being on the field hurt us. Also, my senior year I was a team captain and I was setting a terrible example for the guys on the team.

In hindsight I can see that I was a really emotional young man. I can see that I was immature for sure. But I never associated my bad habits on the field with being immature or selfish. I just didn't link them to my attitude. Of course I don't condone the way I acted but at age 17 and 18 years old I never would have listened to someone my age telling me what to do. On some level, I guess one of the only ways to truly understand that you can't behave that way is to do so and to suffer the consequences at some point.

Fortunately, other than getting kicked out of games and maybe embarrassing myself, I didn't suffer major repercussions for the way I acted. Football was even going to give me the opportunity to go to college.

***

The idea of playing football in college just kind of happened. As I explained before, I spent much of my high school career not being very good, and when you combine that with our team not being very good, I didn't get recruited many places. However, I did believe I could play somewhere.

I spent time in the library looking at college catalogues and settled on the idea that I'd try to go somewhere in Texas.

In the deep recesses of my mind I probably would have wanted to go to Baylor at the time because it was only about 30 miles from where I lived. I never was in the running for the University of Texas or some of the bigger-name schools.

I visited Prairie View A&M but I didn't even talk to the coach for some reason.

Officially, I got invited to visit two schools, Texas A&I, which is now Texas A&M University – Kingsville, and the University of Houston. The invite to visit Houston was on my prom night, so I didn't go to that, so playing at Houston was out.

That left Texas A&I, and I have a great story about my visit there involving a man who would eventually become my friend and rival in the NFL.

A man by the name of Sid Blanks, who played running back at A&I and then for the Houston Oilers, was responsible for my recruiting visit. He took me down there to show me the campus and to introduce me to some people.

Eventually I met the head coach at the time, a man by the name of Gil Steinke. Coach Steinke seemed like a nice guy and he brought me to the dorms to meet one of his star players, a big, tough-looking guy named Gene.

Well after Coach Steinke introduced us he wanted me to get to know Gene and some of the guys, so he gave Gene five dollars and told him to take me out for the night and to show me a good time. Back then you could drink a lot of beer for five dollars so I was ready to go.

When Coach Steinke left, Gene put the five dollars on his bed stand, took fifty cents out of his pocket and tossed it to me.

"You go out and have a good time," he said.

He then rolled over and didn't say another word.

At first I didn't even know how to react. I mean this guy just made $4.50 for talking to me, and I didn't have anyone else to hang out with on campus. I also didn't want to have to tell on him or anything or explain what was going on to Coach Steinke, so I left and didn't talk to either of them. In fact, I didn't talk to Gene again, whose last name was Upshaw, until I played against him in the NFL.

He played for the Raiders for many years, won a few Super Bowls, went to a bunch of Pro Bowls and eventually became the head of the NFL Players' Association.

I teased him about that visit almost every time I saw him. I'd say, "What'd you do with that $4.50, Uppie?" And he'd just laugh.

After I got back from that trip a gentleman who my mother worked for as a maid took me to North Texas State University to visit. I had become fond of the school when I was looking at those catalogues and I wrote the coach a letter about how I'd like to play there. From what I understood they looked at some film of me from the schools we played, liked what they saw, and invited me to campus to meet me.

The moment that sticks out most in my mind from that trip is right when I was going to meet all the coaches. I was wearing jeans and a sweatshirt with the sleeves cut off that day. That was the cool look back then and I remember feeling confident walking down one of the hallways at the athletic facility towards the coach's office.

As we got closer I could see through a big window that all of the coaches were in there. Now, being the kind of kid I was, and wanting to make a good impression, I began to think that maybe I wasn't big enough or strong enough to make the team. I don't know why, but I was insecure about stuff like that.

So what did I do?

I excused myself from the man who was walking with me down the hall, and I went into the restroom and I knocked out as many push-ups as I could. I must have done forty or fifty push-ups straight. Why? I wanted to get a pump going so I'd look bigger for the coaches. I couldn't go in there without sleeves and my arms looking all skinny. No way.

When my muscles looked good and full, I waited until I caught my breath and went back to the man I was with. We proceeded to walk towards the room and I could see that the whole coaching staff was there. It was a small room, maybe ten feet by ten feet.

I knocked on the door and all the guys jumped out of their chairs to meet me. Then they offered me a scholarship right there on the spot. It felt fantastic.

I was all set to play on the freshman team the following year for Coach Ken Bahnsen.

CHAPTER 3
JOINING THE MEAN GREEN

True to my form at the time I got in a fight with my roommate on the first day of practice. I don't remember for the life of me what it was about. Neither of us got hurt and nothing carried over, but we had a big dust-up over something and really went after it for a while.

The thing I remember most is that once it was over, we had to share a ride down to the practice field from the dorms and we didn't talk the whole way; not a positive start to my college football experience. But things would quickly turn around as I learned how different college football was from high school.

When we got to the locker room I saw that we had an actual chicken coop as a locker. I mean there was literally nothing special or even altered about it. It was a 100% old chicken coop. It was about twice the size of a small bathroom and they made the freshman get in there and I thought it was unique.

Then I quickly forgot about my fight and the chicken coop with what happened next: I saw my equipment. For the first time in my football playing life, everything I had was brand new!

I had new shoes. I had a new practice jersey. I had a new helmet that fit my head properly.

I know these are things most kids take for granted now, but no way, not me. To me, having those things made everything else I'd gone through that day all good.

Then I went up to the practice facility and they had a water station for us. That was amazing to me. We never had a drop of water in practice when I was in high school. We had nothing there.

I know it's hard for some kids today to imagine, with mandated water breaks and coaches knowing the value of hydration and things like that, but when I played in high school, nobody knew about that stuff. If you needed water you were considered weak. If you were thirsty, it was much better to tough it out than to be the one who asked for a drink.

But North Texas had a water station so maybe they were enlightened on that point. Either way, with my new gear on I was ecstatic – that is until practice started and I realized we'd be doing all kinds of drills.

I was the kind of young man who loved playing football, and by that I mean the game of football itself. I could play it all day every day... But I was never a big drill guy early in my career. It's not like I wouldn't do them or refused or anything, I just didn't like them very much at the time. I didn't understand the technique and all the things I could learn yet, so for that first practice I did what I always did once things got underway. I attacked the ball every chance I got and the skills that I had seemed to work just fine on my new college teammates.

What I didn't appreciate at the time, but what definitely prepared me for my time in the NFL, was the conditioning and strength building that we did. I wasn't a strong weight lifter, but some of the training that we did added much-needed power and endurance to my game.

We did one-hundred yard relays pushing a two-man sled, where you'd take it 50 yards and then you'd wait until somebody else brought it back before you can finish it. We also did 50-yard duck walks almost every day, which helped me work on balance, foot positioning, hip strength and thigh and lower leg power.

I also learned some humility.

One of my North Texas coaches' favorite drills was bull in the ring. I know some schools don't even do it anymore, but it was basically a set up where a player would be the bull and then there would be six or seven guys around him in a circle, making the ring. The coach would call the jersey number of one of the guys in the ring and he'd charge the bull. If you happened to have your back turned to him that's too bad.

We had this little guy on our team, Red Spence, who was a middle linebacker. On either my first or second day, Red was the bull and they called me to rush out there and block him.

I didn't think anything of it because he was so much smaller than me, so I ran in there very confident that I was going to take Red down. Man, was I wrong. Red came at me with his forearm and dropped me straight to the ground, knocking me out cold. Boom.

All I remembered when I got up was the headache. I know I should have been embarrassed about that, but I wasn't. I took it in stride and realized that I could never underestimate anyone at the college level. It was a good lesson to learn, one that would come back to me in my early days with the Steelers.

After Red took me out, I said to myself over and over again that I didn't have time to feel sorry or sulk. I had to strap it on and get back in the ring. I had to move past it. And that's what I did.

Another thing I did was eat more food than I ever had in my life.

***

When I got to North Texas I maybe weighed 238 pounds and they had me slated to play middle line-backer. By springtime of my freshman year I was up to 265. I will never forget my first experiences with the dining hall. I had never seen anything like it and I had never had access to that kind of food.

So, you couple the availability of endless food and my increased physical workload with college ball, and I was eating constantly. I used to start off break-fast every single morning the same way:

4 donuts. 4 eggs. 6 strips of bacon.

Before my meal was over I'd have had about a half-dozen eggs, a half-dozen donuts and maybe another six pieces of bacon.

The only clothes I could wear by then were the bigger T-shirts in my closet. I had blown out everything else. I also ate myself out of a position.

When the coaches saw how easily I put on size and kept most of my quickness, they moved me to the defensive line for my sophomore year and that's when I really started to thrive.

I got Sophomore of the Year and Defensive Lineman of the Year that season and I was feeling pretty good about the team. I was having fun and for the first time in my career I was a part of a winning team.

My junior year was interesting because I had to deal with something I'd never experienced in my career to that point: injuries. In the second or third game I hurt my ankle and kind of hobbled through the next few games until I hurt the other ankle and no matter how hard I pushed, I couldn't practice after the games. My ankles wouldn't let me and eventually I had to get boot casts on both ankles.

I could still walk, but the casts caused all kinds of problems; some funny, some not so funny.

One of the funny things I had to deal with was that the boot casts had about a 4" heel on them. You combine that with the fact that I was already 6'4" and one of the bigger guys on campus, and all of a sudden I was hobbling around school looking like a monster standing darn near 7' and weighing 270 pounds.

I used to have to walk near an elementary school to get to the coaches offices and one day I was hobbling along while the kids were out on recess. Well, they took one look at me and probably thought I was Frankenstein or something because they all ran!

All I could do was laugh. I was quite a sorry sight during the week with those casts.

I say during the week because I wore the casts all week and then they'd take them off Saturday morning so I could play in the games, then they'd put the casts on to stabilize my ankles after. It was a crazy process and it worked very well, except the one time that I got tired of the casts and decided to take them off myself with a fork.

Yes, a fork.

I tell this story as an example of the kind of foolish, impulsive thinking I was capable of back then. I truly have no explanation for why I took off my own cast early other than I wanted to go to a party. Whether this party was anything special or not, I don't remember either.

What I do remember is sitting in my dorm room on a Friday night, standing half in the shower, running water over my cast and chipping away at it with a fork to get it off. Even telling this story feels absurd, but I did it.

I spent Lord knows how long in that shower soaking the cast and hacking away at it, all so I could go to a party. That's just the kind of foolish thing I did back then...unless I had a great time at the party. Maybe I did. I don't remember, specifically.

It went like that for me my junior year. Playing. Putting on the casts. Playing again. We had a strong year. I think we won seven games.

I ended up having surgery after that year and then becoming a preseason Playboy All-American before my senior year.

That experience is one thing I'll never forget. They flew me to the Chicago Playboy Mansion and I hung out at the Playboy Club with the Playmates and all the other All-Americans that year, including a running back out of the University of Southern California named OJ Simpson.

Nowadays the All-American level guys have seen each other at camps and traveled together and met each other on social media, but back then, this was the first time I'd met some of the guys I'd only seen play on TV. I met Bob Babitch from Miami of Ohio and Ron Pritchard from Arizona State. I got to spend time with Jake Scott from Georgia and some other guys I'd get to know later in the NFL.

When I got back to campus I was thinking, "Okay, Joe. What are you going to do now? What have you done for your team lately."

***

The expectations for our team heading into my senior year were sky high. And now that I had spent time with the best of the best in college football, I really began to believe on a personal level that I had a chance to play professionally.

The first time I ever considered playing pro football was during a physical education class in my sophomore or junior year of college. Our teacher was being real positive about how well we were doing and he said something like, "You guys are doing great. You know, you have a real future in teaching if you want it. You could be making yourself $6,000 right out of school."

Well, I had just read that a middle linebacker from Illinois had recently signed on with an NFL team for $50,000 and that conversation with my PE teacher settled it. I was not teaching. I was going to make it to the NFL.

There was also a guy from North Texas who had made it to the pros a few years before me and around the time I had my conversation with the PE teacher he showed up on campus with his nice big car and my mind was made up.

Now, just because I made up my mind that I wanted to be a professional football player didn't mean it was a sure thing. But that Playboy All-American team put me on the radar nationally and I was willing to do anything I could to ride the momentum to a pro career after my senior season.

Of course, we had to play my senior season first, which turned out to be one of the best seasons in North Texas history. We went 8-2 and only lost to Arkansas and Tulsa. Unfortunately, I think we could have gone 10-0 and we were never on anybody's list for a bowl game, but we had a lot of fun that year.

Our last game was against Wichita State and we had a great day. We sacked the quarterback a bunch. We stopped the run. Our defense scored some points. Yeah, we had a terrific day. It was a fantastic end to my college career.

And just like that, my days at North Texas were over. By the end of December I was no longer on scholarship and no longer getting a stipend. I was on my own with my wife and my son waiting to find out if I'd get drafted into the NFL.

CHAPTER 4
WELCOME TO PITTSBURGH

I thought for sure I was going to be drafted by the Philadelphia Eagles. I don't recall if I read that somewhere or someone told me that information, but that was where I envisioned myself landing. I wasn't happy about it because I wanted to stay in Texas. At the time, I would have preferred to play for the Cowboys.

In addition to the team being in Dallas, which was close to my home town, I had really become a big Bob Lilly fan over the years. Lilly had gone to Texas Christian University, now known mostly as TCU, so he played his college ball in Texas like me. He also played defensive line and was built similar to me. I think he was 6'4" or 6'5" and weighed around 260, like me. And he also led the NFL in sacks, so I thought if I could learn from him and if I could get off the line quickly like he did, I'd be all right.

The places that I remember I specifically didn't want to go were Buffalo, New England, Green Bay and, I know how it sounds now, but Pittsburgh.

I just didn't want to deal with winters, mostly, and all those places get cold.

But back then it wasn't like it is now. Nobody was putting a camera in my face or asking me on social media what team I wanted to play for. I guess most people knew OJ Simpson was going to Buffalo, who had the first pick, but after that I don't remember hearing much about where I might go.

I also didn't fly to New York City for the draft. In fact, I didn't even watch it. I listened to it on the radio and found out that the Steelers drafted me from a phone call.

Back then that was it. On that call they told me someone would come down to meet me soon to let

me know what I had to do. I had no idea when that
would happen, so I hung up and wondered what I
should do.

Two days later I came home from the grocery store to
find two men sitting in my apartment, one of them
smoking cigarettes and drinking my Smirnoff vodka.
Nobody locked the doors in those days, but I was
still surprised to see two guys in my place.

Before I could say anything, one of them stood up
and said he was Bill Nunn, a scout for the Pittsburgh
Steelers. Nunn was a sportswriter for the *Pittsburgh
Courier* and Chuck Noll invited him on his staff.
Things would come full circle many years later when
I became a scout and we were able to share stories
and get to know each other better. He was a good,
well-liked man and the Steelers scouting room is
now named after him.

As we became friends later in life, I used to always
joke with him that he was lucky to be in one piece
because I should have taken him apart when he
came into my place unannounced and drank my al-
cohol.

"Man, I should have kicked your butt," I'd say. "You're lucky I didn't throw you out with my bare hands."

We'd laugh about it because these days nobody would just go into your place and wait for you. That was simply a different time.

After my initial surprise, he told me all the information that I needed to start my career as a Pittsburgh Steeler.

***

The beginning of my official involvement with the Steelers took place in what felt like a blur. After a short holdout on my part, I flew from Dallas to Pittsburgh, got off the plane and went straight to the Roosevelt Hotel, where the Steelers offices were, and I met with Dan Rooney.

I don't know if Mr. Rooney was the President or Vice President then, but I remember that the Chief and owner of the Steelers, Mr. Art Rooney, who was also Dan's dad, was across the hall.

Dan and I sat down and started negotiating and I said, "Well, OJ Simpson is getting paid something like $400,000 to run the ball, how much are you going to pay me to stop him?"

We then went back and forth on numbers and eventually Dan pulled back from his desk and looked at me. I didn't know what he was doing, so I looked straight back. Silence. Then he stood up.

"We've been talking like this for a good little while now, and I think we're close," he said.

I don't remember exactly how far apart we were, but it was enough for me to draw a line and not budge anymore.

"Well," he said, standing up. "Why don't we go across the hall and see what the Chief says.

"OK," I said.

We walked across the hall and entered Mr. Rooney's big, spacious office. He looked at us and asked what the problem was. Dan said that we'd been negotiation for a while and we seemed to be at an impasse, but we're very close.

"How close?" Mr. Rooney asked.

"Close," Dan said, and then told him the number.

"Give it to him," he said.

And that was it.

Mr. Rooney then leaned back away from his desk and opened up a small humidor he had in a cabinet. He grabbed a cigar and handed it to me.

"Have a cigar, my boy," he said, smiling.

We shook hands and just like that I was officially a Steeler.

No sooner had the ink dried on the contract a few minutes later when Dan said, "C'mon, we're going to camp."

We had about a thirty-five mile drive out to Latrobe and when we got there the players had just finished lunch, which gave me time to head to the locker room and change. When I got out onto the field and found my position coach, they had woken up the entire offensive line from their naps to go one-on-one with me. Needless to say, they weren't happy.

My position coach on the defensive line took me to the offensive line coach and they lined me up against the starters on the offensive line from left to right.

"Let's see you do some pass rushing," he said.

There must have been five guys waiting to block me, but one by one they lined up and I beat them.

"Line up over the center," the offensive line coach would say.

Then I'd beat the center.

"Over the guard," he'd say.

Then I'd beat the guard.

And on down the line it went. I beat everyone. I don't know if they were pissed off or tired or just didn't care.

Then the second group came in and the coach wanted me to do the same thing. I knocked the first group down easy and I thought the second group would go down no problem as well. Nope. The first guy whipped me and took me to the ground. That man's name was John Brown and he had just been traded to the Steelers from the Cleveland Browns. He was a veteran player and we eventually became roommates.

"Man, what happened?" I asked him.

"Yeah, I hit you," he said. "I wasn't going to let you beat me. I watched everybody you lined up against. I could tell that once you got going I wasn't going to stop you. So I knocked you down at the line."

After I got off the ground one of the coaches approached me and said that now they were going to find out what kind of shape I was in.

"I want you to run the width of the field four times for one set," he said. "So over and back and then over and back again. That equals one. Got it."

"Sure," I said, trying to do some quick math in my head to figure out how far I'd be running. I stopped counting after I got to a mile.

The width of the field is over 50 yards. I think I did the set twelve times. I'll never forget it, too, because during the first few runs a dad was by the fence with his kid, who was probably ten, and the kid was all over me.

"C'mon! C'mon number one draft choice," he said. "Where were you last week? C'mon, number one. Let's go, Mean Joe!"

He messed with me the whole time, and it looked like the nickname I got in college, based on our team, the "Mean Green", had carried over to the NFL.

***

Early on in camp I also learned about the even-temperedness and greatness of my new coach, Chuck Noll.

As I've said before, when I was younger I had a temper and had a bit of a bad attitude about things, especially when things didn't go my way.

In this particular story the thing that didn't go my way was very inconsequential, but it caused me to react how I did and it was a valuable lesson for me.

The way our training camp was set up, the practice facility was in one place, while the locker room was kind of far away and the dining hall was in the opposite direction. When we would get off the practice field, the typical thing to do was to go over to the locker room and take off your gear, get showered up and then head in to lunch. Then you'd relax for a while and go to the locker room to get dressed for the second practice.

I noticed that some guys were grabbing their fresh practice gear and heading straight to the dorm rooms to relax, without bothering to change in the locker room at all. One day I tried to do that after I had lunch and since the timing was off, the equipment guys were now at lunch and the door was locked. Nobody was around to open it, so I kicked the door in, got my practice gear and went up to my room to rest between practices.

I was taking a nap when all of a sudden the door opened and it was Chuck. I knew he must have heard about the locker room door and I braced myself to get chewed out by my new NFL coach. But it didn't happen.

"That will be $500, Joe," he said, and then shut the door.

He said it matter-of-factly and calmly, without a hint of anger in his voice.

I paid the team the five hundred dollars and that was it. He didn't say another word about it and I never heard another word about it. I learned then and there that with Coach Noll, there were consequences to your actions and there was no arguing or yelling to be done.

If you broke the rules or you broke a door, you paid and life goes on.

But you know what? From that day forward, even after they fixed the door, the locker room was always open.

I thought that was amazing. He gave me an appropriate punishment but also understood where I was coming from and ordered the doors to be left open. There were lessons to be learned on both sides of that and they were learned without a whole lot of discussion or debate. Of course, I shouldn't have kicked down the door in the first place!

I am so grateful to Coach Noll. His mannerisms and the way he coached and the things that he *didn't* say helped me go in a different direction than where I was probably headed. I was full of fire when I was younger and I was volatile and if I had a coach who was the same way, I don't know how it would have worked out.

Coach Noll held me accountable for my actions and for my temper and he let me figure out on my own that I was hurting the team. He respected me and coached me at the same time. I spent my life in football and, trust me, that is a rare feat for a coach to genuinely pull off. Many coaches think they can do it, but they can't.

Here's a great example of how Coach Noll knew exactly what buttons to push when he wanted someone to see things from a different perspective. In this case, that someone was me.

We did a lot of losing my first year in Pittsburgh and it brought out all of my old bad habits. I would scream and yell at the officials. I'd yell at everyone. I'd take losing out on whoever was around with my bad attitude.

One game Coach Noll pulled me aside and he said, "You know, Joe, these officials are fathers. They're husbands and sons and friends. Do you think they like being screamed at by you? They're trying their best to do a job. Do you think it makes it easier on them if you're yelling in their face after every call that you don't like?"

I remember that speech really hit home with me. Until then I never once thought of officials as regular people. I know that sounds insane, but they always seemed like a necessary evil to me. I hated how they could decide a game or a play without even having pads on. Chuck humanized them for me and it opened my eyes a great deal.

The other thing that changed my attitude a bit was the simple questions he'd ask calmly during a film session.

We'd be watching tape and after a bad play I'd go on a rant and cost us another fifteen yards and Coach

Noll would say quietly, "What did we gain from hand-ing the other team fifteen yards of offense?"

The way he phrased it is so important. He wasn't yelling at me or screaming that I had to control my temper. He asked a simple question of me, a defen-sive player, about how my actions benefited our team.

As time wore on that season, I gradually began to notice how negatively my attitude affected the team. I came to the conclusion that I was hurting the team on my own. Not only were my tirades costing us yardage on the field, but they would make my team-mates play out of sync. My actions took away their focus on what they had to do and I was ruining our camaraderie. I took us out of the flow and I could see it right there on the tape.

Slowly, I took control of my temper and harnessed it between the whistles. I truly don't know if that would have happened as quickly or at all with a different coach.

I know I jumped ahead here a bit, but I think it's im-portant to understand the influence that Coach Noll had on me that year. People forget that we were 1-13 my first season. That's a lot of losing. But I'll get to that soon. For now, back to my first training camp...

***

I didn't have a real deer-in-the-headlights experience until our first preseason game, when I moved over to the right side and it was an entirely different world. My goodness, I couldn't even find the football. I froze most of the time and when I did move I was often in the wrong place. I was letting myself get psyched out, too.

Before the snap I'd hear the quarterback calling out our entire defense and I'd think, "Man, how does he know our defense."

Then he'd snap the ball and everyone was moving so fast. It was quite different than college. Most of the time during that first game I didn't know who was hitting me. I couldn't tell if it was a running back or a center or guard. I had no idea. It was all a blur of colors.

When I was coaching many years later I'd talk to guys before their first game and I'd say, "Hey, it's going to be a blur. It was a blur to me because my eyes couldn't focus yet. You can't see the game, yet. And if you try to pause for a moment to let your eyes focus, you will get knocked out or blocked or taken down. You need to go as fast as you can, react the best way you can, and let your eyes adjust to the speed. When your eyes adjust to the speed, you'll start to see things differently."

The hard part for me was that I had modeled my game after Cowboys' great Bob Lilly and Deacon Jones when he was with the Rams. Those were the guys I watched the most on the defensive line and one of the things they both did so well, Lilly in particular, was that they got off the ball incredibly fast. They'd come off the ball right at the snap and I did the same thing at North Texas, where I had a lot of success following their pattern.

Early on in practice and in the preseason I got discouraged from using my quickness off the ball because I would get trapped constantly. They would wham me, sucker me, trap me, influence me and basically confuse me every which way they could. And even when I'd beat a guy clean sometimes he'd grab me just as I was getting to the quarterback and he'd be strong enough to delay me or hold me back. That stuff never happened in college and it was frustrating.

At first I spent a lot of time trying to figure out what was going on and that slowed me down both mentally and physically. By the time I was reading what was happening the play would be over. What I figured out was that I needed to run through all the scenarios of what can happen in a play before the ball is snapped.

I had to learn to recognize the location of the backs and what they can do, what the possibilities are, what they could potentially do to me, and if there was a low probability of them coming my way then I was good to go. You simply cannot react quick enough if what happens on offense is a surprise to you, so don't let it be a surprise. So much information can be gleaned from watching tape to find tendencies of what the backs and tight ends do in certain formations. You have to anticipate where they're going to go before the play even starts and your first step has to be towards where they're going to be, not where they are.

The coaches worked with me on learning how to recognize all of those things. Every day in practice they'd go over all the formations that the upcoming team had that could be a danger to me. We called them 'key drills'. During the key drills we'd go over every angle and block that could possibly come my way during a play and I'd practice how I'd handle all of them.

Another thing that helped during practice that year was that I got work in at several different spots on the defensive line throughout the week. First I'd be in front of a guard, then a tackle, then over center and on and on. That way I got to see the different angles and openings that could happen during a play. My whole vision changed. There were different gaps, different blocking lanes and tackling lines.

The benefits of this were twofold. First, I'd gain valuable information about how the offense was going to progress from a given formation. Second, the coaches could line me up at different spots on defense occasionally. This made me more valuable because we could change things up and the offense wouldn't know where I was going to be on a given play.

It was a lot to handle in a short period of time but the bottom line is that it helped me play faster.

By the time we got to our first game against Detroit I was feeling like I belonged, but I don't think I did anything special. I actually remember very little of that game other than we won. I do recall thinking that we had a potentially decent team, but we also had plenty of guys who weren't that good and we had a lot of turnover week-to-week. That year, and the next year to some extent, every Monday or Tuesday after a game there would be a bunch of new faces in the locker room to workout with the team.

On the field I figured most things out on my own or from watching what the veterans were doing. I was there before Terry Bradshaw and Franco Harris and Jack Lambert and all those guys. Ben McGee, a defensive end who had some success in Pittsburgh definitely worked with me on how to handle some of the on-field stuff like dealing with the traps that I mentioned before. He was a tough, hard-nosed guy and he used to say that same thing over and over.

"You've got to trap the trapper," he'd say. "You need to recognize the line-up and see where they are and how they react. Beat them to the place they want to go."

When I close my eyes I can still hear him talking to me about trapping the trapper. He should have had that tattooed somewhere on his body.

***

After beating Detroit, we didn't win a single game the rest of the year. Not one. We lost thirteen straight and finished 1-13.

Unfortunately for me, the losing brought back many of my old habits and my bad temper and poor attitude. I spent much of the season playing the game the way I wanted to rather than playing it the way that would benefit the team the most.

Overall, I was getting better each week and learning from the coaches about how to be an effective NFL player. I just lacked the right mindset to really help the team. My thought process, to the extent I had one, was that I was out there to make a play. I rarely thought about my responsibility to my teammates. I was just playing and running around blocks on the inside and the outside and displaying individual defense.

Oftentimes, when you look out for yourself, even if your desire is to make a play, you put your teammate at risk because you're not playing defense together. You're extending yourself but you're hanging someone else out to dry. Maybe your tackle numbers are high or your sack numbers are high, but those are individual numbers. It wasn't until later on that I understood the ebb and the flow of a team defense and how staying home can be more effective than chasing every tackle. The truth is, as we got better and I improved over the years, my individual numbers definitely diminished. The result? Our team defense got better. And I was fine with that.

What happened to me, and what happens to most guys, is that as you grow and develop as a player, your mentality and approach to the game matures. I began to take personal responsibility for the plays I was making and for putting my teammates in the right position to make plays.

I really owe this kind of personal mental enlighten-
ment to Coach Noll. He always talked about
responsibilities. He'd say, "God, country, family and
football. That's the perspective you need to keep."

While we only won one game that year, I bought into
what he was saying. Then as other guys who would
eventually become household names joined the team
they bought in as well.

***

On a personal level, I was twenty-two years old and I
had a wife and two children. My second son was
born during my first season in Pittsburgh. While I
felt all of the responsibility as a father and as a husband, I didn't carry the day-to-day responsibilities of
raising the babies because my wife stayed in Dallas
near her family while I was in Pittsburgh during the
season.

We talked on the phone all the time and she wrote
lots of letters to me letting me know how she and the
kids were doing. It was very tough for me to be away
from them and I know it was very, very tough on her.
We had two children under two and that is not easy.

It certainly helped that she was with her folks, but for much of the year I was in Pittsburgh focused on doing my job and providing for us.

I relied on a bunch of my teammates to give me a sense of normalcy outside of playing football since my family was in Texas. One of the wide receivers on the team, Roy Jefferson, was really great to me and other young guys on the team. He and his wife Candy would invite us over for dinner and things like that. He had a great family and was a good guy to be around.

John Brown, an offensive tackle on the team who I mentioned earlier, also looked out for me a bit. He was my roommate my rookie year and had probably been in the league for about ten years at that point. He lived very close to the stadium and he and his wife would have me over for dinner as well. If I had to point to one guy who really had a mentoring role for me that year, it was John Brown.

"It's good to have that aggressive attitude on the field during games," he'd tell me. "But you've got to leave it on the field and you've got to control it."

If I got into it with an official he'd be the first guy to tell me that I shouldn't act that way on or off the field.

The funny thing about it, considering what we'd eventually mean to the city of Pittsburgh, is that at that time, off the field we were basically anonymous.

Most of us could walk down the streets without anyone stopping us. We'd go into restaurants and nobody would say anything. If someone stopped us in a bar it usually wasn't to say anything nice. They'd often think that because we were so bad on the field that we were easy to mess with off of it.

There were a few times where we'd go out to have a few drinks and someone at the bar would try to start problems with us. It wasn't fun. We kind of had a target on our backs for the wrong reason. I remember one time I went to a bar and stayed only five minutes because I knew nothing good was going to happen from me being there.

"Hey, are you with the Steelers?" a guy asked me.

"Yeah," I said.

"Oh, I bet I could kick your ass then," he said.

I didn't say a word to him and walked right out. There were lots of comments like that during my rookie year and at the time, it all added up to me not really wanting to be in Pittsburgh.

I hate to say that and I know how it sounds now all these years later, but for a twenty-two year old kid from Texas, it was a tough adjustment.

The sky was always grey and with the steel industry still going you'd have mornings where soot was all over everything when you woke up. There was also that smoky, steel smell that hung in the air.

The thing is, all of that probably would have been okay with me if we were winning. The losing basically magnified all the things I didn't like. The more we lost the worse I felt. Then the Pittsburgh winter and weather came in and that first year I wasn't happy. Even our locker room, which was in the basement of the first aid building for the fairgrounds, irritated me.

My locker was against one of the outside walls, which were made of brick. The brick behind my locker had broken down and water and wind would get through. One game in late November I was getting dressed and there were icicles in my locker. Icicles!

I thought, 'man, this can't be pro football'.

CHAPTER 5
PEAKS AND VALLEYS

My second season in Pittsburgh was filled with glimpses of how good we could be as a team, but plenty of frustration and anger at games we gave away. I should have known the kind of year it was going to be from that very first game. It was a microcosm of what was to come.

We played on the road in Chicago against the Bears to start the season. Our defense was strong all game long and we took a 15-3 lead into the fourth quarter. With about two minutes left, our running back got hit in the backfield and fumbled the ball. A Bears linebacker picked it up and took it to the end zone for a touchdown. Now it's 15-10 with maybe one-and-a-half minutes left to play.

We get the ball back after the touchdown and the Bears blitzed on the first play. And doggone it, the linebacker gets deep in the backfield, hits our running back and he fumbles again and for the second time in a minute a defensive player for the Bears picks up the ball and runs into the end zone. Now we're down 15-17 with maybe 30 seconds left to play and the game is over. We tried a few throws on offense but nothing happened. We lost.

That kind of stuff just ate me up. I'll never forget the anger that surged through my body as the clock ticked down. When the Bears took a knee at the end of the game, I turned the other way and I was so furious about the loss that I threw my helmet as far as I could...and it hit the goal post.

I'd never thrown a helmet before but I really gave it a ride and then bang, it hits the post. I wasn't trying to hit it. I was mainly trying to get rid of the anger and disgust I had for how we finished.

The funny thing about that story is that after the game, nobody said anything to me about my behavior and after a while I had forgotten about it. Many years passed and then on the day I walked into Mr. Rooney's office to tell him that I was going to retire, he brought up another incident out of nowhere.

"Joe, you remember that day you threw the football in the stands in Philadelphia?" he asked.

"It's been a while, but yes, I remember," I said.

"You know," he said. "I felt the same way. We should never have lost that game."

All I could do was smile. By that time we had won four Super Bowls. We'd done plenty of winning. And here he was telling me that we'd been on the same page about hating losing the whole time. It was a great retirement gift.

Of course, during that '71 season I never could have foreseen our future success. We were not a good team then. We were inconsistent and erratic.

We'd lose one, win one, lose two, win one. After losing to the Bears we beat Cincinnati and San Diego and then lost to Cleveland and Kansas City. Then we beat Houston, lost to Baltimore and then beat Cleveland. It was back and forth with no momentum. One game we'd play great defense and the next game we'd give up 30 points. There was just no consistency.

Even within the games themselves we were erratic. We'd get a sack and then a penalty. We'd pick off the other team and then fumble the ball. Seemingly every time we did something good, something bad would happen.

I have to give Coach Noll credit here because throughout all of it, he was a rock. He had key numbers he was trying to get us to reach every week that he believed if we hit, we had a chance to win the game. He never wavered from those numbers.

The numbers were basically a list of things that a defense could do to increase their chances of being successful from one down to the next. For instance, he'd always say that if you minimize the gain on first down then you put the opponent at a disadvantage on second down. So we'd keep track from game to game how many times we'd hold the opponent to three yards or less on first down.

Then we'd keep track of how many times we'd hold them to no gain or very little gain on second down, to make sure our opponent was consistently dealing with 3rd and over 5 yards to go. Third and five or more usually meant they had low odds of getting a first down.

We tracked these things every week and the numbers didn't lie. When we didn't have the key numbers in our favor, we'd lose. In those days, if a team threw for over 300-yards, that probably meant that you were behind and were going to lose the game. One of the biggest factors in having a successful defense in my era was holding your opponent to under one hundred yards total rushing. Back then if you did that you were very likely to win.

Still, we'd sometimes do everything we were supposed to and at the end of the day we'd lose. Coach Noll was so low-key and even-keeled no matter what. He truly believed that if we consistently had his key numbers in our favor, over the course of a season, we'd come out ahead and we'd be a winning football team.

I have to admit, for much of that year, I doubted him. I think a lot of guys did, which meant we weren't buying in because we were skeptical. One thing I learned from playing under Coach Noll and coaching all the places I did is that you can't have skeptical players. Everyone needs to buy in to the team's philosophy or you can't win. It's that simple.

"We're going to continue to work to put the odds in our favor," he'd say. "We need to do the simple things consistently well. Protect the quarterback. Run the right routes. Don't fumble the ball. And make sure the big play works for you and not against you. There's going to be one or two big plays in a game and we need to have the odds on our side to make sure the play is for us."

Little by little during that season I'd notice patterns in our meetings that proved to me that achieving his list of numbers was a good indicator of our success. Even in games we'd lose, I realized that the quarters where he hit our numbers, we were ahead of our opponent. There was evidence that if we followed his plan we'd have a chance to win. Towards the end of the season, he had started to sway some guys, including me. We just needed better players.

CHAPTER 6
THE TURNAROUND

There have been plenty of books and articles written about Coach Noll, how our Steelers Dynasty was built and our super team in the 1970s. Having been there at what I think was our rock bottom, the 1-13 season my rookie year, I can say with confidence that there are two main reasons we became winners.

Coach Chuck Noll is reason number one.

Bringing in talented players is reason number two.

Mr. Rooney hired Noll in 1969, right before I got there. He had been the defensive backs coach under Don Shula when he was with the Baltimore Colts. I remember hearing that Mr. Rooney interviewed Joe Paterno of Penn State as well, but he ended up hiring Chuck Noll.

From 1970 to 1974, we drafted or signed almost a dozen guys that would become household names. Terry Bradshaw, Mel Blount, Jack Ham and Franco Harris joined us in '71 and '72, and then we had one of the greatest draft classes in NFL history in 1974, drafting four Pro Football Hall of Famers in our first five picks: Lynn Swann, Jack Lambert, John Stallworth and Mike Webster.

All four of those guys would win four Super Bowls with us.

For me, the big change came when we drafted Franco. Terry was terrific but Franco made it all happen with his attitude and his performance on the field. He changed everything for us. Back then it was a running league and you had to have a dynamic runner and for many years we had what I'd say was the best in the league.

I think it's important to talk about how attitude can affect a team for a moment. When you have a bad attitude it tends to carry over and things never seem to go your way. On a football team, that usually translates to losing close games on a larger level. On a smaller level, a negative mindset leads to close calls not going your way, penalties going against you and an overall negative momentum.

Franco's attitude had such a positive effect on the team and the offense that when he joined us we started winning games I know in past years we would have lost. We also beat quality teams by playing well. We didn't need flukes or penalties or other teams to have bad games for us to win anymore.

By the middle of 1972, we were getting to the point where we believed that if we played well, we'd win. That was a new feeling for us as a team. Being able to rebound from a loss was new as well.

We lost a tough one to Dallas in the third or fourth game of the season that in my first two years could have easily led to a run of losses. Not anymore. We ended up winning every game the rest of the year except one. We beat good teams, too. We beat the Chiefs, who had been in the Super Bowl recently. We beat the Vikings who had also played in a Super

Bowl. The last three games of that season before the playoffs we held our opponents to five points total.

Five.

We shut out the Browns, held the Oilers to three and held the Chargers to two. Man, that felt good. The last win against San Diego gave us the Division title and an 11-3 record. That was the first time the Steelers had ever won the division in their whole history.

It was a really, really great feeling. Barely two years before we went 1-13 and now we were division champs.

Our first playoff game was at home against Oakland and it became one of the most famous games in history because it ended on the Immaculate Reception. I realize how miraculous that catch was, but that game was a straight up dogfight.

People forget that prior to the final play, the score was 6-3 and we fought tooth and nail for every single inch on that field. The score was 0-0 at halftime and neither defense was giving anything up.

Personally, when I think of that game I think of squaring off against Bob Brown, also known as Boomer.

Boomer stood about 6'5" and it looked like five feet of that was his legs. He had these high hips and long legs and long arms that went down to his knees. He also used to tape his hands and forearms with so much tape it looked like plaster. He was the absolute meanest offensive lineman I ever played against and probably the toughest too.

When we were watching tape and getting ready for that game, we noticed that he was executing his G-block and wiping people out. It looked like he was hooking. They had this play where Boomer would block down on top and the guard would pull outside. When he'd block down, he would take out all these guys with his taped up thumbs and hands and it looked like he was hurting them.

I saw that in the film room and I said, "Oh no, no way. That's not happening to me."

I knew he had to have a 'tell' when he was going to do that play so I kept watching tape and watching tape and watching tape until I finally saw it.

What I eventually noticed was that when Boomer was coming straight at you he was in a narrow, staggered stance, with his left foot way in front of his right foot. Then he'd come across and WHAM! He'd take you out.

If he was coming across, his feet would be more parallel and so I was ready for that block.

When it came to the actual game, I made sure I knew where he was at all times because he wasn't specifically the guy lining up in front of me. It was a difficult assignment, taking on one guy while keeping an eye on another, but it paid off.

They ran the play we watched in the film room three times and all three times I got out of the way the second I saw it coming. No way was I getting taken out like that.

Meanwhile, every play I'm hearing grunting and scuffling next to me.

"Ugh."

"Umph."

"Ooof."

I finally turned to LC Greenwood, who was making all the noise and I said, "What's going on?"

"Man, that son of a gun Boomer is killing me," he said.

"Oh, come on," I said. "Move here on the tackle and take my guard. I'll move out there and deal with him."

The next play I lined up against Boomer and I'll never forget it. I got set and stared into his helmet and there was something off in his face. His complexion was darker than mine and there was something real sinister going on. He had these big red eyes and I could see his teeth and I swear he was growling at me.

"Oh shoot," I thought to myself. "This is a big, angry man."

They snapped the ball and I don't remember anything after that for a few seconds. I simply opened
my eyes and realized that I was looking through my
ear hole and the ball was on the other side. When I
got up I noticed that I'd lost a shoe.

He absolutely flattened me.

"LC," I said, when I got up. "You got him."

I don't know how it would have gone for me if I had
to live there all game with him. That was one play
and I didn't want any more of that.

***

We played the Miami Dolphins at home in the AFC
Championship that year. I'll never forget it for many
reasons, one of which was that it was New Year's Eve
day in Pittsburgh and we had a warm weather team
in town and the weather was in the 60s. I was so
ticked off! This was Pittsburgh in the winter! It
should have been fifteen degrees to welcome those
guys up there and give us an advantage, but it
wasn't.

I played very poorly that game and a bunch of guys had the flu, including Bradshaw, who got hurt in the first quarter and didn't come back in until the fourth quarter. It was a tough, tough game for us.

The score was 7-7 at the half, with their touchdown set up from a trick play involving a fake punt.

Then Larry Csonka ran all over us in the second half.

Bradshaw came back in late in the game and actually lead us to a quick score, cutting the lead to 17-21. Then we threw a few interceptions on our final possessions and our season was over.

The amazing thing was that for the first time in my life, I was not devastated with the loss of a football game. I mean, it hurt and I hated to lose, but I couldn't help reflecting on how far we'd come in just a few years - from winning one game my first year to having this kind of success. It seemed impossible.

We won eleven games. We won our division. We won a playoff game. We made it to the AFC Championship for the first time. I was upset we lost but I was pleased. Frankly, it shocked me.

It was a real positive stepping stone and I could see that we had what it would take to eventually win a Super Bowl. We had the talent. We had the coaching. We had the mental grip on how to win in the playoffs.

That last point might be the most important in life and football. I truly believe that you must have mental toughness to succeed in life and the only way to get mental toughness is to overcome adversity. The harder the adversity you overcome in your profession or personal life, the stronger you will become. The more scratching and digging and crawling and clawing you put in to achieve your goal, the better off you'll be.

I didn't know it at the time, but that's what my first two years in Pittsburgh were about: building our toughness and giving us the mental foundation to be able to eventually win a championship.

I even wanted to have a party after that Dolphins game. I didn't have many takers, but that's how good I felt about the steps we took in 1972.

CHAPTER 7
GREAT EXPECTATIONS

One of the beautiful things about playing for Coach Noll was his 'what have you done for me lately' attitude. He was that way with negative things and that way with positive things. If you did something great, he acknowledged it and moved on. If you did something poorly, same thing.

When it came to our season after winning the first division title in franchise history, Coach Noll was the same old guy. He would not let us look back to what we did the year before and he wouldn't let us look ahead to what would happen if we made the playoffs that year. I know it's cliché, but it was drilled into us to take one game at a time. He emphasized that as much as he could.

That mindset is so valuable in football and in life. In both instances, if you're trying to accomplish something difficult and worthwhile, you can be guaranteed that you will fail small things, you will fail big things and you will succeed in big things and succeed in small things. If you let any of those four things affect you too much, you will never get past them.

Having the mentality that Coach Noll had allows you to maintain focus in the face of both tremendous success and disappointing failure. I would say that compared to where the Pittsburgh Steelers organization was when I was drafted, 1972 was a tremendous success. I'm thankful Coach Noll didn't dwell on it for one minute.

When we opened camp the next year, our focus was not on winning the Super Bowl in 1973, though we knew we were a very capable team. Our focus was to have one great practice, followed by another, and to beat the team we were going to play that upcoming week. No more, no less. Win or lose, regardless of what the outcome was during that next season, the most productive thing we could do was to focus on the next practice and the next game. Focusing on the Super Bowl was useless. That game wasn't next on our schedule and you can't play it until you get there, so why fret over it?

"You are not guaranteed a single thing," he'd say. "All we can do is play each game as we face it the best we can."

The way Coach prepared us showed so much leadership that I think every coach can learn from it. His consistent mannerisms and consistent treatment of players kept everyone sharp. I personally believed everything he said because he was always honest and fair and everything he said proved to be true in the end regarding our teams.

I'll jump ahead here a little bit, but when I was heading into the end of my career, Coach Noll called me into his office to tell me he was going to replace me as a starter and turn me into a rotation player.

"Well, Joe," he said. "Once upon a time it was a non-decision about you starting. Now, we have to make a decision."

I was really upset but what he said resonated with me. It made me face the fact that my play had come to a point where I was no longer as good as I thought I was. Of course, I fought and tried to regain my position, but it didn't work.

By that time, between my age and the pounding my body had taken, I wasn't the same player I used to be. All of the wear and tear manifested itself in a lack of explosiveness, a lack of quickness and a lack of power.

I retired after that season and I'll get into my decision to retire more when the time comes, but I bring the story up to illustrate the point that Coach Noll was fair and honest with everyone all the time and we all respected the heck out of him for it.

He was as blunt with a rookie as he was with a guy like me who he'd won four Super Bowls with. He wasn't buddy buddy with his players. He'd pat you on the back after a good play or he'd crack a joke and share some thoughts or stories about life, but that was as far as it goes.

All of that is to say that heading into 1973 we believed we were in the upper echelon of the NFL. Beyond that, Coach Noll treated each of us exactly as he had the year before and the year before that. He didn't blow smoke and he didn't let us get ahead of ourselves from game to game.

Now, on the defensive side of the ball, we knew we were getting good. We liked playing together and we liked trying to shut teams down. I think we only gave up two touchdowns in the first three games of that '73 season. It felt good. At our high point we were 8-1 and had only given up more than 20 points as a defensive unit once that season.

Our low point that year was a three-game losing streak towards the end of the season where we lost to Denver, Cleveland and Miami. In years past that might have put us in a tailspin that we couldn't get out of. By that point, however, we believed in ourselves and how we were playing and we rallied to win the last two games of the season.

This lead to a playoff game against the Oakland Raiders that I wish I could forget. To get ready for that game, we practiced running a defense that we had never played before to try and trick them and they ran all over us. It just didn't work.

Marv Hubbard and Charlie Smith both rushed for over 70 yards on us and they barely had to throw the ball. Ken Stabler probably only had 150 passing yards that day. He didn't need to throw it because they could run everywhere. It was a terrible feeling. We'd come so far from the year before and we had a good regular season and then to lose in the first round of the playoffs was awful.

Coach Noll always said that he didn't believe in motivational speeches or things to inspire players. He believed that inspiration and motivation should come from within; from a desire to be great. Well that loss to Oakland lit a fire inside of me that burned the entire off-season.

I believed that we were a great team and I knew we were going to show it in 1974.

***

We opened the 1974 season by shutting out the Baltimore Colts 30-0. That was a good start to the year. Then, of all things, we tied the Denver Broncos and gave up 35 points in the next game. And we followed that up by getting shut out by the Oakland Raiders in the third game and losing 0-17.

What a swing!

We went from a dominating performance, to giving up a bunch of points in a tie, to being shutout. Talk about experiencing everything the game of football has to offer in three games. As always, Coach Noll's steady hand guided us. He told us to ignore the tie and forget about the shutout and start preparing for the next game, which we did.

From that point on, our defense really played well and kept us in every game. Our offense was growing too, of course, but I was concerned with my side of the ball. Only one team the rest of the season cracked twenty points on us and four times we held a team to a touchdown or less.

Jack Ham had a tremendous year. He had five interceptions as a linebacker. It seemed like he was always finding the ball. I'd be going after the quarterback and sure enough I'd look back and so many times I'd see him causing a fumble or deflecting a pass or being involved with a tackle.

We finished the season 10-3-1 and had to play OJ Simpson and the Buffalo Bills in the first round of the playoffs. We played a predominantly Stud 4-3 that day and held OJ to under 50 yards.

After that game there was a lot of people talking in the media about how the real Super Bowl was happening in the other playoff game in our conference, with the Miami Dolphins, who won the last two Super Bowls playing against the Oakland Raiders who had won one as well. The Dolphins were trying to be the first team to three-peat.

John Madden, the Raiders coach, even said that the best two teams in football were playing that day and after they won, he said that again.

In our first meeting after we beat Buffalo, Coach Noll addressed what Madden said as we prepared to face his team.

"People out in Oakland think that the best two teams in football played yesterday," he said. "But you know what? The Super Bowl will be played in two weeks and the best team in football is sitting right here in this room."

When he said that, the case was closed. I knew we were going to win. I believed him and he was right.

I'll never forget the feeling we had coming off that plane in Oakland before the game. We were beyond ready to go. We *knew* we'd win.

We even had a secret weapon ready to go: Ernie Holmes.

Ernie was going to match up against Gene Upshaw for that game and all week long during practice we were messing with him, getting him fired up.

"Ernie," we'd say. "Upshaw is gonna kick your ass."

LC and Dwight would be all over him.

"I'm telling you," LC would say to him, laughing. "Be careful. Upshaw is no joke. He's gonna take you out."

Every day we wouldn't let up.

Finally, we show up in Oakland and we kicked the ball off to them to open the game. The Raiders started with the ball on the thirty-yard line. As we got into our huddle to call the play, Ernie steps away from the huddle and walks towards the Raiders offense.

"Eugene!" he shouted. "Eugene Upshaw!"

Upshaw steps out of the huddle and looks to see who's calling his name and sees Ernie standing there as angry as a bull.

"Eugene Upshaw! I am going to kick your ass!"

Oh, man. He was angry.

"You tell'em, Ernie," Dwight said.

And let me tell you something. He kicked butt all day long. It was wonderful to watch. The result was that they only had 29 yards rushing the whole game. We dominated their offensive line from start to finish and with three touchdowns in the fourth quarter we earned the right to play in our first Super Bowl against the Minnesota Vikings.

***

The famous sportswriter from the *LA Times*, Jim Murray, interviewed me in the week leading up to the Super Bowl and my mindset from the Oakland Raiders carried over.

"We're overjoyed to be here," I said, referring to the Super Bowl.

He thought I was saying that we were just happy to be there, but I wasn't. We came to win it. It's simply what I believed. In fact, we were all so confident we had a great time in New Orleans getting ready for the game.

We ate a whole lot of New Orleans cuisine and rode boats and visited Mel Blount's family. It was a very enjoyable time. None of us were nervous at all.

The only person who had it rough was Dwight because he got sick early in the trip and stayed in the hospital until the morning of the game. He went right to the field from the hospital and his knees nearly buckled after a few practice hits, but he played the whole game, even getting our first score, which was a safety.

That game was all about defense. It was 2-0 heading into halftime and then 9-0 heading into the fourth quarter. Neither team could get much going in the air. Bradshaw threw for 96 yards and the Vikings quarterback, Fran Tarkenton, threw for 102.

But where we really made our mark was in stopping the Vikings running game. Their leading rusher was Chuck Foreman with 18 rushing yards total that day. That's it. We would not let them breathe. Our goal was to keep them to zero yards on the ground and we darn near made it.

And then, just four seasons after going 1-13, we won our first Super Bowl.

Euphoria. Euphoria. Euphoria.

When that clock finally wound down it was absolutely euphoric. I can't think of a better word for it because that's what euphoria is supposed to be. Total joy.

We had spent so much time at the bottom of the NFL. Then when we finally became a good team we had tough losses in championship games and even a disappointing season to follow it up. To finally bring one home was the greatest feeling an athlete can have.

And then when you share it with the fans and you see their reaction to what you've accomplished, it goes to another level. When we got back to Pittsburgh it felt like every bridge and every road was filled with people as we drove. It was probably 18 degrees outside but thousands and thousands of people were there, hanging out of their windows and cheering us on.

It was the best feeling imaginable.

I celebrated that feeling all the way until the first day of training camp the next year.

CHAPTER 8
GLORY AND LEGACY

As I mentioned earlier, there are many excellent books and documentaries about our Steelers teams that I have enjoyed being a part of and that I know fans would like.

My four Super Bowl wins as a player and the two we won when I was a special assistant with the Steelers are among my proudest professional accomplishments. As I reach the point of winning our first Super Bowl while telling my story, however, my mind doesn't wander to the next three Super Bowls, each of which were wonderful in their own right.

Rather, I find myself jumping from memorable moment to memorable moment in my career, where I learned a valuable lesson or witnessed true character or leadership.

For instance, when I think of that first Super Bowl win, I am proud that we did it the right way, with integrity and hard work. A moment on our journey that stands out to me took place in one of the few years prior to our championship, when we were playing the Houston Oilers.

As we were preparing for that game, one of our locker room attendants found a playbook that the Oilers had left behind. He brought it to Coach Noll, who quickly called a team meeting.

A few minutes later, Coach stood in front of all of us and held out a binder.

"Gentlemen," he said. "This is the Houston Oilers' playbook. We play them twice this year. We have all their plays and their game plans."

Then Coach Noll held out the playbook and dropped it into the trashcan.

"We're not going to open it," he said. "That's not how we do things. We are going to prepare how we prepare, we're going to line up against them on the field, and we're going to do what we do and that will give us the best chance to win."

Then he walked away.

What an incredible image and statement. Now, I'm not saying that many other coaches wouldn't have done something similar, but in a league where winning is everything and teams will take any edge they can get, to publicly declare that we don't need or want whatever edge having the other team's playbook can give was very impactful.

It was moments like those that made everyone on the team buy in. You wanted to play for a guy who took that kind of moral stance. You wanted to be a part of a team that does it the right way. You wanted to win for a leader like Chuck. To him, the fundamentals mattered just as much in football as they did in life. We lost that game, but we won for having witnessed his decision to not use an unfair advantage.

Act honorably. Be honest. Be a good person. Work hard.

Behaving along those principles will lead to a good life and a good career. And as I've said, I had to work hard on many of those things I just mentioned.

There were certainly times when I left some on the field as they say, in terms of practice. It's hard to admit now but when I look back, I wasn't nearly as into the weight training as I should have been. The farther I get away from my career, the more instances I see where I may have left something on the table in terms of preparation. I'm not saying I was lazy at all, but looking back, yeah, there were times I didn't go the distance when I probably should have. It's tough to admit.

When I got into coaching one of the things I preached to my guys, which is what Coach Noll preached to me, was the idea that tomorrow is promised to nobody. All you can do is work as hard as you can today. And on the flip side, there's nothing you can do about something that hasn't happened yet. Don't focus on the next game or the next season. Focus on the now. It's cliché, I know, but it's absolutely the way you need to look at things to succeed. Yes, you need goals, but you set your goals and then you focus one day at a time on reaching them.

Another thing I learned from Coach Noll was that while you had to guide people, you had to let them blossom into their own talent and learn their own lessons. I mentioned earlier how he set the stage for my learning to control my temper not by yelling at me to control it, but by calmly talking to me about the results. Not once did he reprimand me or demand I get my rage under control. If he had, who knows, maybe we would have butted heads and I'd have been traded.

What he did so brilliantly was he planted the seeds for me to come to my own conclusions.

He also didn't over coach me, which is a real problem nowadays, especially at the youth sports level.

As a coach later in my career, I made it a point to teach a player what their responsibilities were on the field, where they needed to be and what they needed to be thinking about. I was also very careful to not tell them the exact way to do it. I never wanted to restrict their natural abilities. Most of the men I would work with reached an elite level of sports largely on their natural skills and work ethic. I know it's an ego thing with many coaches, but sometimes the best thing you can do is not tinker and let a kid figure out how to be more effective.

I even saw this happen with my own sons and the sport of baseball. They both had powerful, natural baseball swings. They could really hit. Then I saw what happened to them as they got into little league and beyond. The coaches started tinkering and tweaking and pretty soon, all of their natural ability was gone. I was quite disappointed in that.

Both of my boys loved playing football as well. They weren't as large as me and probably didn't have the attitude I had while I was playing, but it brought them joy, which is another aspect I'd like to discuss here.

***

Not only did I find football to be a blueprint for life, but I also found it to be beautiful, like art in a way. A few years after my playing days were over, I remember sitting down to watch the Cincinnati Bengals play the Buffalo Bills in a playoff game. The Bengals had this left tackle, Anthony Muñoz, who would eventually be in the Pro Football Hall of Fame, and he was a big, tough guy. The Buffalo Bills had Bruce Smith, who I believe to be one of the best defensive linemen to ever play the game. He was a monster.

I remember it was freezing out and there was ice on the field. I sat down on my couch and got very comfortable because I knew I was in for a treat, watching those two go at it. It was beautiful, that's the only way I can describe it. To watch Bruce extend himself to get around Muñoz, to watch Muñoz counter with different stances, different hand placement, with different footwork... Then to watch Bruce react with his body positions and swim moves and bull rushes. It was a physical chess match with two of the smartest, best players in football. I don't recall who won that game, but it was a masterful performance by two virtuosos and I could not have enjoyed it more.

And that leads to another aspect of the game that I loved: competition.

I loved to play against the best to see how good we truly were. When we were lining up against the great offensive lines of our day and the great backs of our day like OJ and Earl Campbell, you knew you had to raise your game.

That's what I loved about football. At that point there was no more talking to be done. No more BS to deal with. It was your best against their best. If you lost those games, it hurt, but you felt like you weren't walking off the field as a loser, rather, as someone who lost. That's a tremendous difference that only equal competition can bring out.

Those games also highlight the aspect of teamwork more than any other match-up. If there is a talent disparity, then it's easy to imagine one team winning because the other team simply wasn't fast enough or strong enough to compete. The team with greater talent can win without perfect execution and team-work.

But when teams are equal, everyone has to play their best individual and team games to succeed. For in-stance, when you see an exceptional touchdown pass in a championship game against two evenly matched teams, most people celebrate the receiver or the throw. I like to take notice of the whole play.

Each lineman had to block successfully. The running backs had to draw the defense a certain way and pick up blocks. The receivers not getting the ball had to run perfect routes to clear a passing lane. And then, after all that, the quarterback had to read the play right, throw a perfect pass, and then the receiver had to make the catch. That's a long chain of events that had to occur for that touchdown and none of them could have happened alone.

When you appreciate that aspect of the game, all of the "look at me" stuff that goes on with guys seems silly. I know I'm an old school player, but I believe that in a competition you never try to show up your opponent. You don't try to disgrace them or disrespect them.

Even though I got into my individual fights over the years, it was never about disrespect. I know some people will see it differently but that's the way I felt about it at the time. There are certainly instances over the years, especially early in my career, where my behavior could have been seen as disrespectful and I realize that now. Those are some painful memories for me because that was never my intent. Part of maturing is understanding that your actions have repercussions.

It's another hard thing to admit, but I clearly behaved selfishly early in my career as well. Being selfish lets your teammates down as much as it lets you down. Fortunately, football can help you overcome selfishness, especially when you're playing for someone like Coach Noll.

You can yell at someone for being selfish all you want, but more often than not, that's not going to prevent them from being selfish. They need to see that other people's ideas and thoughts matter and that a greater result can be achieved when everyone works together and looks out for each other.

Case in point: our weekly game plan meetings. Early in the week we would come up with an idea of what we think we can do against an opposing team. Oftentimes, especially on a team with a staff of talented coaches, you'll have several different opinions on the best approach and the best strategy. Occasionally, you'll have very strong differences.

If you approach those differences with the mindset that someone is saying you're wrong and that you have to prove you're right, nobody wins. But if you have the attitude that you're part of a larger team trying to get to a great game plan, then suddenly confrontation becomes collaboration.

What ends up happening in the second instance is that you approach the same goal from two different angles and a better plan is formed. You can only have that happen if you're willing to separate your ego from the job that needs to be done. I've seen too many guys disagree about something just because it's not their idea and they want credit. Then nothing gets done.

The way I've always looked at ego is that ego is the little guy that pushes you and motivates you. And as long as he stays the little guy, things are fine. But if he becomes the big guy and he's sitting on top of your shoulders and he's in your head and putting words in your mouth, then ego is in the wrong place.

Ego also prevents you from leaving your comfort zone because as loud as egos can be, they are fragile things. They don't want to be hurt and they don't want to be challenged. They will do everything to avoid a situation where you might make a mistake.

I believe that you have to make mistakes to succeed. You have to fall on your face. That's the only way to forge a fighting spirit. Character is built when you get back up. Character is having the humility to try a new strategy, even someone else's strategy. That's not admitting defeat or failure. It's admitting growth.

I've said these same things to my children throughout their lives as well.

Be true to yourself, be responsible and don't cheat or take shortcuts. If you make a mistake, own up to it. Lying only makes things worse. It shows disrespect for you and for the person you're talking to. That goes for doing homework or memorizing a playbook. Lying about putting in the time does no good because eventually you'll be found out.

As a parent, I set very clear rules with my kids. Follow the rules or there will be consequences. And no matter what, I made sure I was consistent and fair

when enforcing a punishment. I got that one from
Coach Noll, too.

When I was with Pittsburgh there was a standing
$50 fine if you were late for a meeting. I went years
without being late and then one time towards the
end of my career something came up and I was
about five minutes late.

"Fifty bucks, Joe," Coach Noll said.

"Coach, I'm never late," I said. "I've never been late
my whole career."

"Well, you have a history, Joe," he said.

"What do you mean?" I asked. "I was late one time."

"From now on, that's a history, isn't it?" he said.

I shrugged and gave him the fifty bucks. He was
right and I respected it because I knew he would
have fined me the same as a rookie as he did that
day, regardless of how many Super Bowls we'd won.

When you add up all the little rules that teach responsibility, you end up with a philosophy. That was

part of Coach Noll's philosophy and I carried it over into parenting.

I always tried to be consistently fair. I always told my kids to be trustworthy. That was my biggest thing. If you've lost trust with someone, you've lost almost everything. What else is there?

I also tried to keep things simple for them. I believed that if I could instill honesty in them, then everything else would follow suit. If you're honest, then you won't cheat yourself. If you won't cheat yourself, you're unlikely to cheat others. If you don't cheat others, you'll gain respect. It's all related and I began preaching it as soon as they were old enough to understand it.

My wife and I used to always say, "If you let them get away with stuff when they're little, they'll try to get away with big stuff when they're big."

Setting guidelines teaches discipline and I can honestly say I learned almost all of that from football.

In the locker room I was in with Pittsburgh, we had characters from A to Z, but the focus was on getting the job done and accomplishing the same goal. It's the same thing with kids. Your kids are going to have different personalities as well. They still need to learn the same playbook about life.

I learned my playbook from too many men in football to count. I learned from Coach Moore in high school, Coach Rust in college and Coach Noll in the NFL. I learned so much from my teammates and fellow coaches. I even learned from coaches like Tony Dungy and Don Shula long after my playing days were over. I've never stopped learning, in fact. That's the beauty of football and the beauty of life.

Never stop learning.

My hope is that now you've learned a little bit from me as well.

CLOSING THOUGHTS

I've been a football player or working in football most of my life. I played for thirteen years, coached for seventeen and worked as a special assistant for another nine years. I've always viewed myself as a football player by profession.

Though I tried running a few restaurants, I'm not a businessman. I'm not a community leader or a politician or a preacher. I never held the notion that just because I played football and made a decent salary that I knew everything.

I wrote this book to share what I've learned in the

game of football and to discuss how it has affected my life in so many positive ways.

While I wanted this book to stay focused on football and the impact it had on my life, I would not have been able to achieve the level of success that I did without a strong woman by my side the entire way.

That woman was my wife of over forty-seven years, Agnes.

We met when I was a sophomore at North Texas and the first time I introduced her to my mother I told her we were going to get married. They both laughed, but I knew it the moment I saw her.

Neither one of us at the time had any idea that my job would take me to Pittsburgh and that our lives for most of the year would revolve around me playing football on Sundays, but Agnes took everything in stride and supported me the whole way.

She made sure our kids had a great home and childhood. She made sure they went to church and studied and that they grew up to be good people. I did what I could, but as any pro football player will tell you, there's only so much we can be around for.

It always gave me peace of mind to know that Agnes was running a tight, loving ship at home while I was doing what I needed to do to win on Sundays.

She was selfless in so many ways that I've lost track. I remember that she would even take all the kids out of the house on a Saturday before a big home game so that I could prepare and do what I needed to do to get ready for the match-up. I never once asked her to do that. She just sensed I needed it and she did it for me.

As we began to win Super Bowls and go through our run of success, I will be forever grateful to her for keeping me grounded. I may have been "Mean" Joe on the streets of Pittsburgh, but at home, I had to help out with the dishes and put away laundry and do all the things she expected me to do as a husband and father. I cherish those moments away from the stadium with her and my family more than even our biggest wins on the field.

I say all of this because in the end, whether you're an athlete or not, you have to keep things in perspective. Agnes helped me do that and I loved her for it.

God. Country. Family. Team.

That's what Coach Noll taught and that's how I have lived.

It's simple and it works.

Thanks for reading,

Joe

"MEAN" JOE GREENE

"MEAN" JOE GREENE
SUPPLEMENTARY READING

College Football Hall of Fame Biography

Chuck Noll Pro Football HOF Speech

Joe Greene's Pro Football Acceptance Speech

Official Pro Football HOF Biography

Individual Achievements

Team Records

Awards and Honors

MEAN JOE GREENE
COLLEGE FOOTBALL HALL OF FAME BIOGRAPHY

Charles Edward Joseph Greene was better known by his nickname "Mean Joe" Greene. The 6-4, 270-pound tackle acquired this moniker as a reference to his school's nickname, the North Texas State University Mean Green. During the three seasons Greene played defensive tackle for North Texas, the Mean Green posted a 23-5-1 record.

In his 29 games at defensive tackle, North Texas State held the opposition to 2,507 yards gained on 1,276 rushes. A per carry average of less than two yards per attempt. His collegiate coach, Rod Rust, said of the 1968 consensus All-America, "There are two factors behind Joe's success. First, he has the ability to make the big defensive play and turn the tempo of a game around. Second, he has the speed to be an excellent pursuit player." A pro scout said, "He's tough and mean and comes to hit people. He has good killer instincts. He's mobile and hostile."

He was drafted in the first round by the Pittsburgh Steelers and became part of the "Steel Curtain" defense that won four Super Bowls. Greene is also a member of the Pro Football Hall of Fame, being inducted in 1987.

CHUCK NOLL'S HALL OF FAME PRESENTING SPEECH FOR JOE GREENE – 8/8/87

You know, Pittsburgh is billed as a special place and there is no question about that, and I think I found out today that Canton can be classified as something special and it is something special. To the Pittsburgh Steelers, the 1970s were something special.

It started with a new stadium that somehow changed the atmosphere in Pittsburgh. We went from a little place out in South Park that was not very comfortable, to a glamorous stadium, playing in front of people who were very, very enthusiastic and determined. Getting to do that was really something very special. FDS got involved.... there was a thing called the terrible towel, but it all comes down to winning

two Super Bowls back-to-back. You don't do that
with bricks and steel. You don't really do that with
towels. You do that with people and it is my pleasure
to offer here a guy who is really something special,
Joe Greene.

You know, as I look at all the enshrinees, there is no
question that they are very physical people. They
have played the game physically. They are quick,
they are strong, they do all the things well. But the
thing I think that sets Joe aside from everybody is
his attitude. It is something that you can't do anything to get; it is something that you have deep down
inside. He had all kinds of attitudes, but probably
the best one was that he wanted to play the game
very badly.

Before his senior year I was scouting with the Baltimore Colts and I went through North Texas State. I
had the chance to watch Joe for three years, and the
last time I talked with him there was no question,
this just came through the man, that he wanted a
professional football career. It was a very important
thing for him and that is a prime ingredient. One of
the other ones is he didn't like to lose. Joe didn't

come to us fully prepared. I say this because, when he came into the Steelers organization, he hadn't experienced a 1-13 year and we gave it to him that first year. I think that kind of brought out some of the good attitude that I was talking about - that desire to win even more.

Joe could best be classified as a winner. He was a guy who had great physical abilities; the ability to come off the ball fast, the ability to play low, the ability to play every play to the end. But Joe is one of those guys, one of the great football players who had his antenna out and was really sensitive to the people around him and as a result, I think we played together as a football team. Regardless of what some of the sportscasters may say when they start adding up yards and tackles, you win as a team and you function as a team even greater than that. Joe was very much a factor for us and it is a pleasure for me to introduce Joe Greene.

JOE GREENE'S PRO FOOTBALL HALL OF FAME **ACCEPTANCE SPEECH**

You know I'm not going to pretend that I am not emotional about this. I might get emotional about this. The guys that have preceded me have done really well. It is really tough for me but I am going to give it a go. First of all, I would like to express my thanks to Commissioner Pete Rozelle and all of the other NFL owners for making the game what it is today. I loved it. I want to talk about some of those people that had an impact on my life in the course of 18-20 years.

As I reflect back, I start thinking about high school

and thinking about my high school coaches like
Coach Elliott and Coach Moore. See, I was the big
guy around campus, but my heart wasn't as big as
my body and I really didn't want to play football. But
they made me come out and play. I want to thank
them for not letting me quit when the weather got
hot, the sprints got hard and the work got devastat-
ing. I think it made me a tougher person.

I would also like to talk about my college coaches.
Coach McCain who recruited me from Temple, Texas. Coach Mitchell who gave me a scholarship. You
see when I first walked in, I didn't have a lot of offers
and I was really trying to get a scholarship. I had
heard that you had to make an impression, so I
wanted to make sure the guy responsible for getting
me a scholarship was impressed.

I never did like to work out, but I spent a couple of
weeks working with the barbells trying to get my
body looking good. When I walked into his room, I
had on cut-off shorts and my sweatshirt cut-off at
the sleeves and I was pumped up. I walked in and I
stood on my tip-toes and I kind of flexed a little bit
and he said "you got it."

But there is always mother. Mother... she taught me how to live; how to have respect for other people. She also taught me to turn the other cheek. I learned at an early age you only have one mother.

I'd also like to talk about my wife, Agnes. For supporting me all those years when I wasn't acting my age. For lifting my spirits when they were very low. For relieving the pain we all feel on this earth and then finally for letting me know that "you are not super human, you are no super star you are just a husband. You got to wash the dishes, pick up your clothes and all that other stuff."

And my kids ... Charles, Edward, Joquel. They gave me that strong sense of responsibility. See I am glad they came along at the time they did because I wanted them to love and respect the sport as I do. To understand what it means to see these people back here. This is my business. I want them to know about Paul Warfield, Gale Sayers, Jim Brown, I want them to know about these people, Gino Marchetti, Deacon, Mr. Donovan... I want them to know about Mr. Bednarik.

I want to express thanks to my friends from Dallas, my relatives from Dallas, my friends from Denver, my very dear friends from Churchill, my good friends in the north hills in Pittsburgh. See, you have to have someone to share those things with. And they were there during all the Super Bowls and all the big victories. They made it worthwhile.

In my exuberance, I forgot about a coach back in North Texas, my defensive line coach, who really let me know that football could be fun. Coach Farrell.

And there is Mr. Rooney. The Chief...no one can make you feel more welcome than the Chief when he'd say, "have a cigar boy." You know I still have the first one he gave me when I signed my contract at the Roosevelt Hotel... it may not smoke very good, but it sure does look good. He gave the organization the dignity and the class that it possesses. Dan Rooney who has been as much of a friend as an employer, always took the time to say hello and pass along a little wisdom.

Joe Gordon. There is a guy who has been with me for

a long time. He helped me get through press confer-
ences and taught me what to say to the media. Now
that's important for an impressionable young person,
so Joe thank you.

George Perles. Now George was the kind of guy that
you knew couldn't play just by looking at him. And
he knew he couldn't play, but every time he gave a
pre-game speech and prepared us for the game you
knew he wanted to be out there to play with us. I
want to thank George for opening up the game for
me, to let me slip inside. What is it we are trying to
do, why do I have to be here? I don't think that if
George Perles hadn't been the kind of guy he was, it
is quite possible I wouldn't be having quite the fun I
am right now being the defensive line coach of the
Pittsburgh Steelers.

And I certainly do want to thank Dan Radakovich for
putting L.C. Greenwood in the line-up in 1970.

L.C. He was quick, fast and he did everything that
you would ask him to do. I leaned on him a lot. I was
just big, he was quick, so I used his legs. Thank you
L.C.

You know this is the tough part for me here. These guys are something special, Fats ...they will always be that to me. They are frozen in time and I can keep them there. Fats, Mad Dog, Killer, Vanny, Fernie, Capt. Andy, the Old Ranger, there's Wags and Mr. T. That is the way I see them. Lambie, the Hammer, there's Donny and Loren, and then there is Supe.

Supe, my roommate. I got a lot of strength from him. The little country boy from Georgia had a lot of heart and a lot of character. Then there is ...well you move-over to offense and you got Bubba Brown, you got the Mooner, you got Brad, you got the Big Hummer, you got Swannie, you got Stall, these are my boys here. You got Rocky, Randy, Kolby, Webbie, you know who these guys are. And then there is the 12th man.

In Pittsburgh, if you are not at the stadium at 1:00 on Sunday in the fall, you are at the wrong place. The Pittsburgh fans are always there. I remember them most vividly in the 3rd quarter when LA was getting into us pretty good and they were chanting, "Defense! Defense! Defense!" Lambert made the interception. Bradshaw got his hands on the ball and immediately got it to Stallworth and got one of the greatest plays I think in Super Bowl history. Without the fans it is something different and we certainly appreciate and love you for that. And you have impacted my life because you are important.

You know basically what the Hall means to me, coming in with Jim, Larry, Lenny, John Henry, Don and Uppie, well, you know that this is where I want to be. Basically, I am a fan at heart. I admire these people because they have stood the test of time. When it got tough, they showed up to play. They made the contest worth watching because they rose to a new height. I am glad I am here because this is the big event and I love it.

Thank you.

OFFICIAL PRO FOOTBALL HALL OF FAME BIOGRAPHY

A 1968 consensus All-America at North Texas State, **Joe Greene** was Pittsburgh's No. 1 pick in the 1969 National Football League Draft. Almost from his first game, the 6'4", 275-pounder showed the super-star talents that established him as the defensive foundation in Coach Chuck Noll's program that produced four AFC titles and four Super Bowl victories in the 1970s.

Playing left tackle, Greene was named the NFL Defensive Rookie of the Year in 1969 when he received the first of his 10 Pro Bowl invitations. He was named All-NFL five times, and earned all-conference recognition 11 straight years from 1969 to 1979. In both 1972 and 1974, when Greene was selected as the NFL Defensive Player of the Year, Joe played a major role in his team's success.

He had a career-high 11 sacks in 1972 when Pittsburgh reached the playoffs for the first time ever. In a must-win game against Houston, Greene recorded five sacks and a fumble recovery that assured victory for the injury-riddled Steelers.

In 1974, Pittsburgh won its first AFC championship and Super Bowl IX. That year, Greene developed the new tactic of lining up at a sharp angle between the guard and center to disrupt the opposition's blocking assignments. Against both Oakland in the AFC title game and Minnesota in Super Bowl IX, Greene was virtually unstoppable. Joe's pass interception and a critical fumble recovery at the Pittsburgh 5-yard-line were major factors in the demise of the Vikings.

Greene was armed with speed, quickness, strength and great determination and, at the peak of his career, could dominate a game almost single-handedly. A natural leader, he captained the Steelers' defensive unit beginning in 1977. Greene opened his career with a 91-game streak that was interrupted by injury in 1975. Durable, he played in 181 of a possible 190 regular-season games.

"MEAN" JOE GREENE

INDIVIDUAL ACHIEVEMENTS

All-League Teams

All-NFL: 1972 (AP, PFWA, NEA, PW), 1973 (AP, PFWA, NEA, PW), 1974 (AP, PFWA, NEA, PW), 1977 (AP), 1979 (PFWA, PW)

All-NFL Second Team: 1969 (NY), 1971 (PFWA, NEA), 1975 (AP, PFWA, NEA), 1976 (AP), 1979 (NEA)

All Eastern Conference: 1969 (SN)

All-AFC: 1970 (UPI, SN), 1971 (AP, UPI, SN, PW), 1972 (AP, UPI, SN), 1973 (AP, UPI, SN, PW), 1974 (AP, UPI, SN, PW), 1975 (AP, UPI, PW), 1976 (AP, PW), 1977 (UPI), 1978 (PW), 1979 (UPI, SN, PW)

All-AFC Second Team: 1976 (UPI), 1978 (UPI)

Pro Bowls
(10) – 1970, 1971, 1972, 1973, 1974, 1975, 1976, 1977, 1979, 1980

TEAM RECORDS

Steelers' Records held by Greene (at the time of his retirement following the 1981 season)

- [Tied for 2nd] Most Fumble Recoveries in a season – **5** (1978)
- [3rd] Most Career Sacks – **66**
- [Tied for 3rd] Most seasons played – **13** (1969-1981)

League/Team Statistical Titles
Sack Title – 1972, 1976

JOE GREENE CAREER AWARDS AND HONORS

• 1972 Defensive Player of the Year (AP, NE, PW)

• 1974 Defensive Player of the Year (AP, NE, PW)

• 1969 NFL Defensive Rookie of the Year (AP, PW)

• NFL 75th Anniversary Team

• Super Bowl Silver Anniversary Team

• 1970s All-Decade Team

• All-Time NFL Team (selected in 2000)

STEELERS YEAR-BY-YEAR TEAM RECORDS WITH JOE GREENE

Year	Team	W	L	T	Division
1969	Pittsburgh Steelers	1	13	0	(4th)
1970	Pittsburgh Steelers	5	9	0	(3rd)
1971	Pittsburgh Steelers	6	8	0	(2nd)
1972	Pittsburgh Steelers	11	3	0	(1st)
1973	Pittsburgh Steelers	10	4	0	(2st)
1974	Pittsburgh Steelers	10	3	1	(1st)
1975	Pittsburgh Steelers	12	2	0	(1st)
1976	Pittsburgh Steelers	10	4	0	(1st)
1977	Pittsburgh Steelers	9	5	0	(1st)
1978	Pittsburgh Steelers	14	2	0	(1st)
1979	Pittsburgh Steelers	12	4	0	(1st)
1980	Pittsburgh Steelers	9	7	0	(3rd)
1981	Pittsburgh Steelers	8	8	0	(2nd)

ABOUT THE AUTHORS

JOE GREENE

"Mean" Joe Greene was an All-American at North Texas and was drafted in the first round of the NFL draft by the Pittsburgh Steelers. He is a 10x Pro Bowler, 2x NFL Defensive Player of the Year Winner, 4x Super Bowl Champion and member of the College and Pro Football Halls of Fame. He also won two Super Bowl rings while on staff with the Steelers.

JON FINKEL

Jon Finkel's books have been endorsed by everyone from Oscar-winner Spike Lee and NFL Hall of Famer Kurt Warner, to Dallas Cowboys Owner Jerry Jones and ArtofManliness.com founder Brett McKay.

He has published with legends who have won a combined 14 Super Bowl titles, 25 NBA Championships, 4 NBA Slam Dunk contests and a Heisman Trophy.

Visit www.jonfinkel.com for the latest news, book and social media information.

CPSIA information can be obtained
at www.ICGtesting.com
Printed in the USA
LVOW12s0057140417
530828LV00001B/63/P

9 780998 627304